The Diary of a Mindful Dog

THE DIARY OF A MINDFUL DOG

Simple Thoughts from a Not-So-Simple Dog

BOB LUCKIN

DeVorss Publications
Camarillo, California

The Diary of a Mindful Dog
Copyright © 2020 by Bob Luckin

ISBN Print Edition: 978-087516-907-1
ISBN Ebook Edition: 978-087516-908-8

Library of Congress Control Number: 2020939142
First Edition, 2020

Printed in The United States of America

DeVorss & Company, Publishers
PO Box 1389
Camarillo CA 93011-1389
www.devorss.com

TABLE OF CONTENTS

ABOUT MURPHY, THE MINDFUL DOG

Murphy is a ten-pound Maltese, Poodle-Terrier mix. He walks like James Cagney, wears his hair like Lauren Bacall, and sometimes looks like Chewbacca. He devours books and anything he can find on the kitchen floor. Murphy believes great music sounds best from his favorite listening spots under the sofa or bed. He never met a squeaky toy he didn't like and believes the shortest distance between two places includes digging.

Murphy's heroes include Gandhi and Robin Williams, but he learns the most from the people he meets. . .like you and me. I'm Bob and I take care of Murphy.

After living with Murphy for a while, we got to know each other so well that we'd try to share our thoughts even though we don't speak the same language. I use words and he barks or uses his some-times annoying yet very effective nonverbal communication skills. Regardless of the odd noises we speak, we still understand each other.

Here's what ~~Murphy has learned~~. . .~~I have learned~~. . .we have learned so far.

OUR FRIENDSHIP

OUR FRIENDSHIP IS LIKE A LADDER. YOU CAN PLACE YOUR FULL WEIGHT ON EVERY STEP. WHEN YOU DO, YOU WILL BE LIFTED UP.

OUR FRIENDSHIP IS NOT FRAGILE.

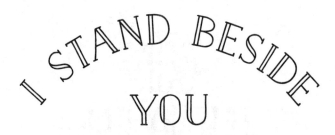

I STAND BESIDE YOU

I may not see the first, or catch the second
of your tears.
I cannot stop them; they belong to you,
as does your smile,
your laughter, and your song of life.

I will walk next to you, if that is your desire.
I will stand by you, and hold your heart with mine.
I will love you the way good friends do.
I will listen when your soul whispers.
I will listen to the heartbeat of your song.

I will feed your dreams and blanket them
with the petals of a rose. I will be there when you
harvest the good that you have planted.

You can lean on me for courage
to remove the stones of doubt and worry.

I will stand by you when you are strong
and during your darkest hour.

I will encourage you to find the words
you need to speak with love and power.

You are here to live your life and dreams.

You are the colors that create the rainbow.

Your heart has wings strong enough
to lift you above the darkest night.

I am your best friend, standing here beside you.

DREAMS

If your dreams fit
in the same kitchen drawer
as my walking leash,
your dreams are too small.

The best dreams will fill your mind,
your heart, the whole neighborhood,
and even further . . .
well beyond our longest walk together.

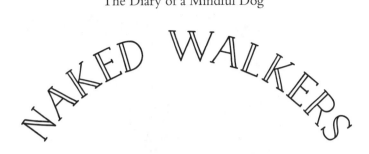

NAKED WALKERS

On my walk I pass people dressed in shame, guilt,
and yesterday's failures. They wear loose-fitting
optimism and hand-me-down beliefs.
Some wear constructive criticism,
judgment, and worry.

I meet those hiding behind plastic dreams
and pretense whose uniforms are monogrammed
with other people's names.

I pass those afraid to reveal their true beauty.

I love the naked walkers,
the ones not hiding from me or from you.

I love the people who don't run away when our hearts meet.

I love the people whose smile encourages the morning sun
to rise, and the evening stars to share their light each night.

ECSTASY
(. . . AND BACON)

My heroes don't quit.
Some get lost, but they don't quit.

Some share other people's wisdom
like cheap boxed wine.
They are doing the best they can.

OTHERS KNOW EXACTLY HOW TO AGE
A THOUGHT,
WRAP IT IN WORDS, AND POUR IT SLOWLY
INTO MY SOUL.

I LIVE FOR THOSE TRUE MOMENTS OF ECSTASY
(. . . AND BACON).

WINGS

PEOPLE DON'T FIND THEIR WINGS UNTIL THE PLACE THEY WANT TO GO REQUIRES THEM.

HAND-ME-DOWNS

IF YOU ARE WILLING TO WEAR HAND-ME-DOWNS AND AN OLD COLLAR, YOU ARE ON YOUR WAY TO INNER PEACE AND TRUE HAPPINESS.

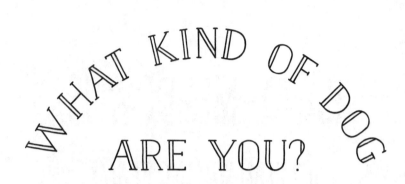

WHAT KIND OF DOG ARE YOU?

The finely dressed man asked what kind of dog I am.
I replied, "I am a dog who has no shoes.
Shoes would make my feet sad.
If my feet couldn't touch the ground,
I would not be able to feel my soul."

Again he asked, "What kind of dog are you?"

"I am a dog with no bed. If I were to sleep
in a bed every night, I would only be able to
dream dreams the size of my bed."

Then, what kind of dog talks to people?

"I am the kind of dog who smiles
when I see your heart, dances with your mind,
and loves you beyond words. I am a dog that can
roll in the mud, make friends with a fox,
a bird, and an owl. I have four legs instead of two
because I have so many places to go.

I can smell a blossoming rose a mile away
and hear the heartbeat of a child's song.
I have no clothes, so I don't have a washing machine,
a laundry room, or closet. I don't have a mirror
to see myself dressed in fine clothes.

I am a little dog with hair growing everywhere.
I love people unconditionally and play more than I eat.
People keep me because they need to be reminded
to discard the things that bind them.

I am a dog who knows how important love is."

The Mole and the Hole

Because I am a dog, I don't have the same fondness
for cats that humans do; but I confess to having
developed a great respect for them. Every morning
a brown cat named Nutmeg leaves the house across
the street, comes over to my yard, jumps the fence into
and back out to the other side so that he can sit about fifty feet
from a hole in the ground.

He sits hour after hour watching that hole.
Twice in the last week I watched a mole
leave the hole as Nutmeg planned his attack.
Twice Nutmeg came within inches of catching the mole.
Nutmeg never said, "Guess I will quit, since I am not much of a hunter."
Nutmeg never went off
to a corner to brood about his past failures.

He never complained to other cats about how
unfair life is. He never blamed his failures
on the weather or other conditions. His failures
were simple failures that had no special meaning.

One day I noticed Nutmeg sitting on a mailbox across the street.
I never saw the mole again.

I could not help but wonder what it would be like if humans
didn't make so much of their successes and failures.
Most of the humans I know make up stories
to explain and justify their successes and failures.

Sometimes I think the stories are just like the hole
that hid the mole. They don't protect the storyteller
any better than they protect the mole.

WORDS FULL OF KINDNESS

I LIKE IT BEST WHEN YOU USE
WORDS FULL OF KINDNESS AND LOVE.
I LOVE WORDS THAT ADDRESS YOUR FEARS
AND EMBRACE YOUR TRUTH.

I SEE HOW THE WORDS YOU USE TO GET EVEN,
OR PUT OTHERS DOWN, STICK TO YOUR HEART
LIKE YESTERDAY'S GUM AND
MAKE YOU UNHAPPY.

WORDS ARE THE CORNERSTONES OF THOUGHT.
EVERY WORD YOU SPEAK HELPS CREATE
A ROAD MAP THAT KEEPS ME FROM
GETTING LOST WHILE I LISTEN TO YOU.

HUMANS
DON'T HEAR

I was fortunate to be at the bedside of a new mom
when she held her baby for the very first time.
As she looked into the babies eyes this is what I heard:

Mom:
Long before you were born I heard your song
hidden between the colors of a rainbow

Child:
I am only small on the outside
There has never been another me
For you my life has just begun
In truth it began long ago
I carry deep within my being
the history of humankind
I am the keeper of tomorrow

and your teacher for today
I have gathered light from every star
Light is my gift to you
I am the dreamer of dreams eager to come true
My life is full of questions that I will answer
Problems I will solve
Mountains I will climb
And gifts that I will share
I don't believe in words like "can't"
I don't believe in failure
I don't have a story that makes me tall
Or walls that make me small
You will not be able to hide me from pain or suffering
Nothing can steal my joy of life
Nor my song and laughter
I am yours and will always be
Thank you for your kindness
And your gift of love for me

HEALING TOUCH

I understand things
humans sometimes forget.
Each time you touch me,
I fall in love with you all over again.
Touch helps heal hurt feelings
and disease.
Your gentle touch is worth more
than a thousand of your best words.

SOMETIMES

I FEEL LONELY

My life is good. I am living it well.
I am grateful for what I have,
and for all the love I receive.

Sometimes, I just feel lonely.
I am not sad or depressed.
I don't need sympathy.

Some days my life is like a layered cake without the frosting.

Sometimes when I am alone for a day,
I long to see a smiling face.

I want to feel you're loving hand gently touch my neck.
I don't need words or promises.
I just want you to understand.

Sometimes I feel lonely, and your touch
is a lot like frosting.

Seasons

People talk a lot about
the change of seasons.
I see the seasons change between
morning and night. They change after
morning coffee and when people smile.
They change when people fall in love
and when they discover they have never
been alone. There is no season too warm
or cold for the heart.
Every season is a season for love.

LIFE ON THE OTHER SIDE

Last week I attended a funeral.
Everyone seemed sad.
I heard a someone say, "May he rest in peace."

On the way home I asked Bob what he was thinking.
Before he answered, I noticed him smile the biggest smile
I have ever seen. This is what he said:

"Once dead, the last thing I want to do is rest.
I want to travel to the moon and stars.
I want to reflect on the past, look into the future,
and ride my bicycle with the wind at my back.

Once dead, I want to write cosmic novels,
and learn how to play the piano.

After lunch with Robin Williams,
I want to walk with Jesus and Ernest Holmes.
I want to talk to people who didn't believe
they would live after their body died.

I want to take art lessons from Michelangelo
and acting lessons from Burt Lancaster.
I want to skydive without a parachute,
and run alongside a cheetah.
I want to rub the belly of a leopard.
I want to swim with a thousand dolphins.
I want to catch the spark of light in a stallion's eye.
I want to watch people fall in love
and be kind to each other.
I want to communicate with every living creature.
I want to watch angels grow their wings.
I want to listen to the first song a baby sings
and play with puppies."

Marinated in Time

Pat smiled as she extended her hand.
Humans shake hands, I lick.
As my wet nose and tongue gently touched
her soft worn skin, I could feel her heartbeat.

After nearly a century of life, her hands still held
the memories of all her children and every creature
she had ever loved. Feeling her strength
and compassion for others set my tail in motion.
As a dog, I can sense kindness
and I could tell she's lived a good life.

I hear people talk about the aged as if they were
table scraps of memory. You can't tell the true age
of a person by looking at them.
The heart and soul doesn't wrinkle with age.

All creatures have a heart song.
Dogs have a special gift.
When we look into your eyes
we hear your heart song, and sing it with you.

The song your heart sings
has no date of birth, or ending.

TENDING THE FIRE

MOST PEOPLE KNOW HOW TO LIGHT A FIRE.

I WANT TO STAY WITH THE ONES
WHO KNOW HOW TO TEND THE FIRE.

EVERYONE I MEET IS A HERO

Everyone I meet on my morning walk is a hero.

None are prepared for the life they will live.
Each will stretch and learn as they create their life.
Each will conquer demons of unimaginable size.
Each will grow weak in the knees when love opens their
heart. Each is writing a life story.

Some will live and die and be known by only a handful
of other walkers. Sometimes I wonder if everyone I meet
is alone on the inside. I hope not. People need to
connect, love, and care for each other. That's the unseen
substance of life. It's a substance that will never die.

I love morning walks. I love meeting the day as it
quietly opens the hearts and souls of those who cross
my path. I love morning smiles. I love the chorus of birds
excitedly celebrating the day. I love the time just before
folks rush to get to the end of the day.

One more thing. . .I also love the sound of the door
to the cabinet where Bob keeps my treats.
I always get one after the walk.

27

Not a Dog Person, eh?

On my walk today, I heard two people talking.
One said, "I'm really not a dog person."

The other one quickly responded with,
"Well, I don't like cats, so I guess I am not a cat person."

As I thought about it, I could not help but wonder:
How does a person become "not a dog person"?
What could possibly have gone wrong that would make a person
turn completely against puppies and dogs?

I began to wonder if humans who dislike dogs
also dislike humans with large feet or small heads.
What about people with large ears or small noses?

I can't dislike a fellow dog because of the color of his eyes, nose, or fur.
When I meet someone who's not like me,
I figure they must be alive for a good reason, living a life worth living.
I can't imagine how life would be if I had to come up with
a checklist or something to help me to decide if they're
good or bad, likable or not likable.
My nose can only smell where they've been, or what they just ate.

At my house, we think people of different shapes, sizes, and colors
are just fine.

It's so much fun when they visit. I'll admit, I get a little excited
when I hear them at the door, or see them walking up the driveway.
But that's my way of letting them know how good it feels to see them.
I can't help it. That's when I start wagging my tail as fast as I can.
And guess what? They always smile!!
Sometimes, they even get down on one knee and rub my belly.
Oh. . .I really like that.

Honestly. . .how can anyone, NOT be a dog person?

BECAUSE YOU CAN

Love because you can.

If love needs an explanation, Make up a story about it later.

Love now.

CHOOSE

YOUR WORDS

I listen when you talk to others.

I even listen when you talk to yourself
(you should see yourself).

I love it when your words empower, inspire, encourage,
warm the heart, and awaken in you a passion for living.

I love words with soft edges, words offering comfort
that need no apology.

I love hearing words that expand your mind
and encourage questions.

Your words define yourself,
and they help others understand themselves.

I watch as you carefully wrap them
and give them as gifts to those you love.

Choose your words carefully.

I am not a little dog.

I think people see me with their eyes instead
of their imaginations, so they think I am small.
People with imagination know that when I run,
I have to slow down to keep from flying.

Bob and I use our imaginations all the time.
For example, Bob told me every night he talks to
every cell of his body and thanks each one
for the work it has done. He tells the cells
they no longer have to age by default, but that they
can age by decision. He has decided to age
backward to the age of forty-two and has
instructed his body to make it so.

People who know Bob tell him he is looking younger.
Maybe they are using their imagination,
or maybe things get their start in our imagination
and over time become real to those around us.

I think imagination is the private workshop we use
for creating things that will one day become public.
In my workshop, ants march, crows never stop talking,
and pigeons are unpaid sanitation workers
who clean up after humans.

My imagination never gets old.

RISK

THERE ARE SOME CATS AROUND HERE
WHO LIKE TO WALK ON TOP OF THE FENCE
JUST OUTSIDE OUR WINDOW.
WHENEVER I SEE THAT, I START BARKING
REALLY LOUD TO MAKE THEM JUMP.

I'VE NOTICED HOW CATS ALWAYS LAND
ON THEIR FEET. HMM . . .

. . . I wonder if they jumped before they discovered that fact.

People often discover their gifts after they jump. Success seems to have more to do with a willingness to jump than to assurances of landing on your feet.

My Life Is a Grand Safari

I get really excited about venturing out beyond my home,
where the world is changing from day to day.
Bob calls it an exercise walk, but to me it seems like everyone
is either blindly talking on a phone or listening to music instead
of enjoying the beauty all around them. I want to see
what's out in the world, every step of the way. I call it a safari.

My daily safari is always filled with suspense, joy, surprise,
and adventure. I am so focused on not wanting to miss anything that I
rarely think about the past or the future. I am fully present. Everything I see
is alive with color, smell, and shape.
I am wonderfully surprised by everything.

Part of the excitement is exploring every blade of grass
in case I find something new. Yesterday, I saw what Bob calls
a frog sitting in the middle of our path.

I don't know how he did it, but that thing jumped
all the way to the other side of the path.
His landing ended with a thump and a croak.

I don't think Bob saw the frog because he was walking
for exercise. I had waited my whole life to meet this odd fellow.
He had no hair, no eyebrows, no visible ears . . . and no tail.

I hope you understand why I don't walk for exercise.

My life is a grand safari.

HER NAME IS OCEAN

I love running on her beach and watching the birds
I scare take off just before I touch them.

I love watching her steal my footprints from the sand.

I love her fragrance.

You'd think that something with a refreshing smell
would taste just as good, but not here.

When I first met her, everything about her felt great,
I loved it. But when I tasted her. . .yuk. . .
I learned that lesson the hard way.

Another thing I really like about her is that
she's always in the mood to play.
I don't know what makes her so restless, or why
she never sleeps. I have never seen a creature
that can play for so long. I know she is very much alive.
She likes to steal my tennis balls.

She doesn't seem to have or follow rules
and can't be leashed.
In spite of, or maybe because of this,
people love her, flock to her, swim with her,
and claim her shores.

I think she has a heart like mine,
full of wild energy, mystery, and freedom.

Your Life Is a Gift

Good morning!

This is your morning for dreaming out loud. This is your day to say yes to your inner smile, creative ideas, and heartfelt desires. Today is the day you have been getting ready for. Now that it is here, don't be afraid to roll around in it like I do. Don't be afraid to sing and dance on its edges. Stop listening to yesterday's rented conversations. Don't allow yesterday's struggles and disappointments to make you small. Today is your day to live large. Today is your day to swim in love, embrace the morning light, and allow your toes to feel the earth.

Your life is a gift you were meant to unwrap.
Enjoy and celebrate it with every fiber of your being.
If I am not in the house when you come to visit,
I will be outside rolling around in the grass.

That's what I do. Feel free to join me.

SMILE

THE GREATEST LOVE OF ALL WILL SOAK YOU TO THE BONE AND MAKE YOU SMILE IN YOUR SLEEP.

MIRACLES, MYSTERY AND WONDER

Last night I dreamed that on my morning walk
I discovered the Department of Miracles,
Mystery, and Wonder.

I was pleased to find such an amazing place.

In my dream the sign on the front door kept getting smaller.
One day, as I walked by the office I noticed
the sign was gone, but the office was still open.
As I passed by a voice spoke to me:
"A careful observer does not require a sign.
For many people miracles, mystery, and wonder
will always be the stuff of fairy tales;
for others it is the substance of life that needs no sign."

If Not for You

Remember I told you how sometimes I can hear what humans can't?
Well, one night Bob was staring out the window and this is what I heard:

"If not for you, there would be a place of emptiness
in the heart of God.
If not for you, all the good you have done
would still need doing.
If not for you, the spark of your ideas would not have
ignited a fire in others.
If not for you, the key role you have played in life's drama
would remain unfilled.
If not for you, at least one person would not have
awakened to their dreams.
If not for you, your triumphs could not be
examples to inspire others.
If not for you, someone who needed love
would not have received it.
If not for you, a life would have been shortened,
or never have existed.

If not for you, the song of life would have missed a beat.
If not for you, your gifts would remain un-given.
If not for you, another might have suffered
in your place.
If not for you, someone would have
no path to follow.
If not for you, there would be one less smile,
one less laugh, and one less hug.
If not for you, there would be one less
ember of love to warm the soul.
If not for you, something would be missing.

The heart and the soul of God is within us all."

That's when he stopped and sat down next to me.
I put my chin on my paws and realized: If not for you Bob,
a dog might be homeless right now.
You have always made a difference to me.

Who you are is important to someone, somewhere, every day.

I ATE THE CHICKEN, ICE CREAM, AND...

I once ate the chicken, ice cream, cookies, and French bread on the white sofa in our living room. People really get mad when I eat their food. (Sometimes they don't put it out of my reach. . .but that's another lesson.)

When they discovered what I had done,
they yelled at me and I felt bad and unwanted.
The next day, I watched them clean the sofa and realized
they didn't hate me after all. I heard them explain
to a friend how radical forgiveness is possible only
when the person forgiving has the capacity to love.

I know my family loves me because they didn't
give me away after I ate their food. It may seem
radical to forgive someone who has really hurt you,
but choosing to not love someone ever again
because of something they did is much more radical.

If someone seems angry toward me, I step back and,
if necessary, I drop my head down low and look up with sad
eyes to show them how sorry I am. If someone wants to
punish and hurt me, there is probably a deeper reason for their
anger that has nothing to do with me.

I'm very good at forgiving people. It would be pretty
radical if I refused to forgive them for being human.

The most radical thing I can imagine doing
is withholding love.
It's clear to me that for both humans and dogs,
love is the thing we most need to give and receive.

THE DOG PARK

Today we went to the dog park, one of my most favorite
places in the world. On the way, I got so excited
that I starting pulling Bob by the leash
because he was walking too slow.

I get to play with others and their toys,
and meet new people who think I'm cute.
What could be better, right? Yup, I'm a lucky dog!

But then out of nowhere, Bob tells me it's time
to go home. That's when I make him chase me because
I don't want to go home. Regardless, he corners me
and hooks up the leash for the walk home.

That's when I started thinking about
the extraordinary life I live.

I don't go to work. I enjoy free room and board,
dozens of walks, and I have lots of toys to chew on.
I sleep while others clean and pay bills,
and I get to play and nap whenever I want.

Bob says that every living creature is a blessing.
Each has a spark of the Divine. I looked up at Bob
and thought about what that means.

People at the park spend a lot of time telling each other
what makes their dog so special. For a moment,
I felt sad that I was not able to tell everyone
what makes the people in my life special.

After we got home I laid down
and wondered about all the people that I know,
and if they care about each other
as much as they care about me?

The dog park made me tired.

RUNNING

EVEN THOUGH THE FEARS
YOU ARE RUNNING FROM
MAY HAVE LONGER LEGS THAN YOU,
YOU CAN STILL OVERCOME THEM.

PUMPING GAS

Bob was pumping gas one day
when a woman pulled up next to our car.
I watched from the back window
as Bob offered to help pump gas for her.

She was moving slow and seemed to be afraid
to step away from her walker. As they looked
at each other and smiled, I could tell
that she really appreciated Bob's help.
In a way, she gave him her heart,
and he gave her his.

The two of them danced until her car was all full.
When the pump bell rang they stopped dancing
and she drove off. They danced without moving.

No one saw them dance. . .except me.
It's unlikely Bob and this woman will meet again.

I knew then as I know now, both their lives
had been changed forever. Sometimes the greatest
love of all can be found living quietly in the space
between a good deed and a smile, or peering out
from the back seat of a car at a gas station.

Love knows how to find its way around words.
A single spark of love can disappear from the eye
in a second and live in the heart forever.

BLISS

BLISS IS A SMILE ON THE INSIDE THAT MAKES YOUR TOES TINGLE . . . OR YOUR TAIL WAG.

Running and Barking

People often say that in order to avoid feeling
overwhelmed by life, a person must learn to still
their mind. For some, finding inner quiet may be easy.
For others, they just roll their eyes in frustration.

When you find yourself feeling stressed about
something, it may seem impossible to quiet your mind.
Often when you are in that kind of situation,
you just want to run and get away from it all.

I recommend running and barking.

Just do what I do. . .
Run as hard and as fast as you can.
Run until your legs feel like they're going to fall off.

There's one problem though.
People don't like all the loud barking.
They say it's annoying, and you don't want to do that.

So instead of barking, there are a few other things
you can do to still your mind like. . . singing a quiet song,
taking a bath,
going on a long walk,
working in the garden,
meditating,
or actually going for a run (if you can't run physically,
then imagine yourself running).

I think humans don't realize how much energy
accompanies fear and anxiety. When you find
a physical way to express energy, you are on
the right path to finding balance.

When people see me run through the house
as fast as I can, they think it's funny. Maybe it is.
But for me, it is just one of the ways
I express excitement, love, and fear.

Running and barking bring calmness to me.
You may need to experiment to find
what brings calmness to you.

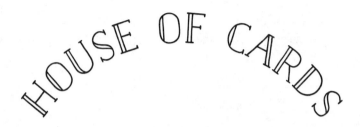

Since I am not human,
there are things I need to have Bob explain to me.
I asked Bob to talk to me about human relationships
and this is what he said:

"The relationship between two people is a house of cards.
There is a trust card, a support card, an intimacy card,
a sex card, a money and power card,
a faith and soul card, and a family card. There is
an adventure card, a courage card, a crises card,
a sadness and loss card, and a grief card.

They all somehow fit together and hold each other up.
No card by itself can do everything. There are no extra
or unimportant cards. When any single card is removed,
the loss is hardly noticeable, but the house is weakened.

If you keep removing or neglecting cards, eventually the whole house collapses, and the relationship falls apart.

Too often humans fail to notice the condition of their house of cards. Most people I know want their house to last a lifetime. Some folks think that once vows have been exchanged and the house is up and standing, it should be able to survive any storm and take care of itself.

The strongest relationship has glass windows that can be broken, doors that must be opened, and doors that must be closed. Lasting relationships require courage, faith, the wisdom of an architect, and the skills of a carpenter."

I loved what he said, but felt bad
that I chewed on his deck of cards.

THE DANCE FLOOR

If there were no tears,
there would be no words for sadness.
If there was no laughter,
there would be no sounds of joy.
If there was no greatness,
minds would have no wings and dreams.
If the heart knew nothing of love,
there would be no love songs,
no people holding hands, no hugs,
and the dance floor would be empty.

The Medicine of Caring

When humans are sick or in pain, they behave a lot like dogs.
Some howl, while others try to hide their pain.
Some snap, while others are able to manage without complaint.
I have noticed that how people feel about themselves
before they are sick or injured has a lot to do with
how they deal with whatever has gone wrong.

The other day, I got an invitation from the hospital to come
and take a look around. They thought a dog like me
could bring some comfort to the sick and injured, and maybe a smile.

So while I was walking from room to room,
I noticed how some of the other visitors were less open to kindness
than the people they were visiting. One visitor told me to go away.
I didn't understand that at all. So I just kept walking around,
cheering others until I finally realized something.

continued on page 62...

Some people may have a fear of hospitals,
or an unhappy memory about a sad experience there.
I saw how a person's past hospital experience could either help
or prevent their ability to be healthy again.

When patients or visitors took time to rub my ears or pat me on the head,
I could feel them letting go of fear. Since nobody there was expecting
to see a dog and a happy tail, it made them stop for a moment
and smile. I think I helped them forget for a while that they were in a hospital.

What I noticed most was the courage and strength of the human spirit.
I watched as hardworking hospital teams of caregivers
wove love and compassion into everything they did.

I saw a family's tears of joy following a successful surgery.
I watched a man who had lost everything regain his dignity and
(with the help of a social worker) find a place to stay.
The best medicine I saw was not in the form of a pill;
it was love without words woven into everything.

Sometimes I get sick and Bob gives me some pills.
He thinks I don't know it because he tucks them in a piece of cheese
or peanut butter (don't tell him that I know the pills are in there).
The pills help me get better, but it's the special attention
and extra care that really helps the most.

SAY THANK YOU

Don't ever pass the chance to walk, run, or
stand and dance in the rain. Stand in it until you are
drenched. Enjoy knowing that no matter how much more
it rains on you, you won't get any wetter.
Sometimes when I get all wet,
I'll shake it off and get wet again!

When the sun comes out, welcome it as you would
a special friend. Enjoy the warmth and all the light
it brings. When night comes, the warmth of the day
will linger in your soul. Lie on the ground and watch
as the sky opens a cosmic dance floor.
Say hello to the moon and greet the stars.

Invite your heart to write a love song.
Allow your soul's whisper to heal you.
Then just before you close your eyes to sleep,
say "Thank you."

Forbidden Food

When I want forbidden food, I know just how to get some.
I sit by the table where the food is being served and watch people eat.

I watch as they take each bite. I watch them chew. I watch them swallow.

Sometimes . . . I even swallow or lick my lips when they swallow.

They usually send me away from the table,
where I wait a few minutes, then quietly return.
The most important step to getting some forbidden food
is to catch the eye of the person I believe who's most likely
to share some with me.

Here's the secret . . . tilt your head, hold the ears up,
all while keeping the eye contact. For most dogs, this skill comes naturally,
but for the young pups it may take some practice.

When my favorite person with food finally breaks down
and feeds me, I behave like I haven't had anything to eat in weeks.
I do not waver, not even for a second.

I pursue each table scrap as though my life depends on it.

MY STRATEGY WORKS

One interesting thing I've noticed over the years
(especially during holidays,
when forbidden food drops like rain from the table)
is how some people can be just as hungry
for the same food as I am, but they are often unwilling
to take a stand and ask for it. . .and actually enjoy it.

Instead, they complain that what they want
is out of reach and would be too troublesome
for someone to pass around the table.

Not me.

I see no trouble asking someone to hand me
a platter of chicken Parmesan.

The way I see it, the path to a well-nourished life
requires a willingness to sit at the table of abundance,
even when others are trying to ignore me.

GIFTS

I can't play the harmonica.

I can't fix the computer.

I can't sing, no matter how much I try.

I can't finish that crossword puzzle.

I can't change the oil in the car.

Every day I hear people put themselves down
because of the things they say they can't do.
The sad thing is, people don't give themselves
nearly enough credit for the things they can do.

For example:
I can wag my tail AND my entire body
all at the same time.

I can hear food being unwrapped
from anywhere in the house.

I can hear you thinking about taking me for a walk
long before you even begin to look for my leash.

I can scare any bird out of here with one bark.

I can make little kids giggle.

I can clean the dishes. . .if you'd let me.

I can tell that you're about to go somewhere without me
when you get those suitcases out of the closet.

Those are just a few of the amazing things I can do.
I imagine there are a thousand things
you do every day that I can't do.

I think you and your gifts are amazing.

Every Great Leader Is a Student

Red, my Irish Setter friend, just finished obedience school. Red's family thought he was untrainable; the obedience teacher thought otherwise.

When the class ended, it was clear Red loved doing whatever was now asked of him. Red's family was impressed by the changes and asked the teacher how she did it.

She explained to everyone, "Some people think they are a good leader because they love their dog. They think being clear and direct about what they want is aggressive. Dogs can't figure out what you want unless you tell them what you want in a way they can understand. Don't sugarcoat leadership."

"Be firm and be compassionate even when Red is not agreeable, or slow to grasp what you want."

Red's family nodded as the teacher went on:

"Love is not a potion you spread over poor communication
to make it easier to understand. Don't love him to get him to love you.
Love is unconditional acceptance of him, his gifts, and his limitations.
A good relationship has clear rules that can be understood and followed.
You are his leader, but that does not mean you won't make mistakes.
Each of us must learn how to lead and follow. A good leader knows
he/she must be willing to learn every day.

Good relationships are demanding.
They can fail when expectations are not clear or achievable."

After the trainer finished, Red's family all looked at one another
with a new understanding of the role they play in Red's behavior.

When they got back home, I could see their car pull in the driveway.
Everyone got out, and while Red was walking beside the car,
he looked over at me and I could tell he had come home a happy dog.

In human relationships, people take turns leading and following.
I think what the dog teacher said applies to all relationships,
large and small.

Now, back to my bone.

LOOKING IN THE MIRROR

Bob was reading this aloud one day,
so I thought I'd share it with you.

"Looking in the mirror, I see the outside of me is changing.
Looking into the eyes of the one in the mirror
looking at me, I see the inside of me is changing.
There is a softening and a hardening."

There is perfection and letting go. There are no places
to hide. The very young and very old will not be enslaved
by those who have lost their fire. You will not find me
on a broken curb or dead-end dream.

Looking in the mirror, I see smiles and tears, laughter and fears,
bumps and lines. The mirror has no clocks or calendars.

I see that I am changing. Years from now I hope to be
an old dog who can look in the mirror and see fire.

YOU ARE A DREAM THAT MUST COME TRUE

Most of you know that Bob and I have long talks.
What most of you don't know is that
he likes to read me poetry. He thinks I don't understand,
but I do. Poetry is heart music,
and heart is something I have a lot of.

Bob has days when he worries and takes negative
circumstances too seriously. One day, I sensed he was
a little down, so I wrote something for him.

I will share it with you because I like to do what I can
to lift others up. I hope my words encourage you:

The days and nights will always be filled with light, dark, joy,
sadness, and everything in between. You bring magic to life.
You bring smiles and laughter that warm the heart.

Love because you can. Laugh until you cry, and cry until
all that is left is your smile. Sadness is a storm that can easily
overcome you, yet it can never stay in one place very long.
Even the greatest storm has no hold on you.

Breathe deeply.
Take in all of life; there is no real joy in shallowness.
A butterfly embraces the same breeze as an eagle,
and a dandelion is rooted in the same ground as the rose.

You are the blossom of possibility,
a dream that must come true.
You are all that the heart and soul
have ever longed to be.

AMAZED

I AM AMAZED THAT WHENEVER
I GET TO WHERE I WANT TO GO,
I DISCOVER THAT
I HAVE JUST STARTED MY JOURNEY.

RUNNING IS FREEDOM

When I am excited and have no place to go,
I run in circles as fast as I can.

My family is just beginning to realize how important
running is to me. When I run, everything changes.
When I stop running, everything looks different.
Sometimes I have to get away from things that upset
or excite me so I can come back and see things
with different eyes.

When I need to see the world around me,
I dance around the kitchen drawer until someone gets
the message and grabs my leash and takes me outside.
There is magic in any action that favors what I have
in mind to do. The action of running says I am going
somewhere and that I have the strength to get there.

When I can't get someone to take me for a walk
or run, I run in my sleep. Running is freedom.

Obedience School for Humans

There should be an obedience school for humans. The first thing they'll learn is that life is to be lived, not managed.

Those enrolled will be encouraged to stop thinking about what they do for a living, how much money they make, and how many important people they know.

Students will learn to run in circles as fast as they can (like I do) and enjoy going nowhere. Successful students will savor life the way I love a good bone.

Students will discover that simple things—like a walk
or playing ball with someone—will give them
an inner happiness. They will grasp the value
of being obedient to love instead of
being driven by power and control.

The advanced students will learn to enjoy the excitement
of hearing the wind blow. They will smile when they feel
the sun's warmth touch their skin. They will marvel at a
bird's song and how ocean waves feel
washing over their feet.

This school will have very few rules. Too many humans
already think that life is all about following rules.

There will be no dogma.
Dogma makes the body stiff and the heart cold.
When they graduate,
they'll know the meaning of play and
will keep their lives simple enough to enjoy.
Graduates will love unconditionally,
laugh a lot, and smile even more.

THE HURRICANE

On a windy day, it feels good to lift my nose,
feel the breeze, and sometimes pick up a yummy smell.
But when it blows really hard,
the wind is no friend of stuff outside.
When the wind gets loud and powerfully strong,
it can make us rethink how we look at the world.

Hurricanes don't bow to the left or right
of old or new opinions.

Wind has no favorite god or religion.

The mighty wind awakens sleeping heroes,
way-showers and dreamers.

The wind can destroy
the strong while lifting the meek.

The wind can tear down
the oldest of walls.

The wind can destroy indifference.

Hurricanes show us how fragile life can be.

Today, like every day, will pass.
What will be lost and found remain a mystery.
If all goes well, I will have a bed to sleep on,
a bone to chew, and fresh water.

I can only hope the outside birds
and trees fare as well.

The Water Bowl

One hot day, Bob was gone for a long
time and he forgot to fill my water bowl.

He's usually pretty good about that,
but this time he must have been
thinking of something else.

It happens.

I got so thirsty that I couldn't keep
my tongue in my mouth.
When he finally got home,
instead of jumping all over him,
I took him over to my bowl
and showed him it was empty.

He knew right away that he
forgot to fill it and apologized.
I could tell he felt bad.

While filling the bowl,
he told me a story about a
kettle . . . whatever that is.

The kettle told the fire that the water
had boiled into thin air, never to return.

A memorial service was conducted
in memory of the water.

Most in attendance were very sad.

Later that day it rained.

I Want to Play

While walking to the dog park with Bob, another dog,
the size of a pony, was barking and trying to bite me.

I found myself asking two questions: Why did he do that?
Can't we all just get along and make this a world that works
for all of us . . . big or small? These are similar to questions
humans have been asking.

When I reached the park, pony-dog had just arrived.
I stayed away and watched with fear as his leash was removed.

He immediately began running in larger and
larger circles, then finally stopped five inches from my trembling,
well-groomed, tiny body. He wasn't barking this time,
but I was still scared, even more scared than when
I get out of the car at the veterinarian's office.

Pony-dog quickly crouched down into his "I want to play" look.
You know, that get-down-on-your-front-elbows-with-your-bottom-up-
and-tail-wagging position that humans think is so cute?

My fear disappeared, and we played for close to an hour.
When I got home, I thought about the whole experience.

I think dogs are on leashes because people are afraid we will
run away, harm, or be harmed by someone or something.
Now don't get me wrong about this. I'd rather not be on a leash,
but I've seen some dogs who haven't come close to earning
the trust it takes to walk around without one.

For me, a leash represents fear and a lack of trust.
Leashes limit access to the free world for dogs, at least until
they've proven they can be trusted. That seems fair to me.

Many humans wear invisible, short leashes of fear and mistrust.
Fear makes it impossible for humans and dogs to overcome
obstacles and allow themselves to grow.

A world that works for everyone is going to require
humans to remove their leashes and assume
the universally recognized "I want to play" position.

I Met Him on My Morning Walk

He was sitting on a thin strip of grass separating the sidewalk from the ocean. I just couldn't ignore him. He told me he was too young to be old and too old to be young, and that he lived in a space between exceptional and extraordinary. He remembered his birth on a morning in 1944 and said, "I am nineteen, except on the days when I am forty-four." I knew he was telling the truth. Nobody makes that kind of stuff up.

He pointed his long wrinkled finger toward a group of clouds that looked like a mountain range and said out loud with a big happy smile, "Those are MY special clouds." He looked down at me and explained, "I collect them. Some have never seen the light of day, while others hide the sun.

Few people know that clouds
are made of joy and sadness, love lost and found,
tender passion, and tears. Thin clouds above the fluffy ones
are dreams waiting to come true. When conditions
are exactly right, a spark of love and light will ignite them."

As Bob and I were about to walk on, I saw him look down
and watch an ant crawl up his long well-traveled leg.
I expected him to brush it off, but he didn't.
"It's taken you a long time to find me,
Charley," he said, in a warm and inviting voice.
"Where have you been my friend?"
It took a moment for me to realize that
Charley was a very large black ant.

Charley stopped, turned his head, and seemed to listen.
Charley hasn't always been an ant. We have been together
many times for many reasons to do things of great importance.

continued on page 88...

The last time I saw Charley he was a sparrow here on the beach. I ate a biscuit and he ate the crumbs. I asked him how he was, and he told me how much he loved his wings.

You may not realize this, but each of us has a rich and complicated history that we neither see nor remember. Our history lives in the background shaping our thoughts, feelings, and lives. You and I will live many lives. Some will start at sunrise and end when the moon claims the night sky.

Some lives will be lived for pleasure while others, plagued with pain and suffering, will change the world. Most will not remember the beginning or the end of the last adventure, nor much about the beginning of this one.

What matters most is that you experience limitless love and joy.

THE SPARROW LANDED

One day I was watching Bob as he stood on the porch
with anger in his eyes. His world had become an angry place.
To my surprise, a sparrow landed on the porch railing.
Bob turned his head and looked into its eyes.
As he quietly moved closer, Bob could actually see
its tiny heart beat and hear its inner song.

Bob looked at me, I looked at him and did what
I usually do. I wagged my tail. Only this time,
nice and slow because I didn't want to scare the bird.

At that moment, I could tell Bob had changed.
He now felt love as it started replacing all the
anger and self-centered fear he was feeling.
Suddenly, all he could see was love and nothing else.

I was amazed at how quickly his world changed.

Awakened

I had a dream last night that an extraordinary event
turned people into dogs.
Suddenly, all wars stopped, there were no more religions, hate ended,
and there was no more talk of one person's god being
bigger or better than another person's god.

In fact, everyone seemed to accept and understand that God
had never been a person, but was in fact
an elegant intelligence throughout the universe.

At first, some of the small dogs were afraid of the big dogs,
but the big dogs could find no advantage in being large
and had no desire to control those smaller than themselves.

Hunting dogs loved to hunt but never showed disrespect
for dogs that didn't. Dogs of the Far North were dressed
for the weather, as were dogs of the Deep South.

There were no arguments about which dogs were the smartest.
Every dog understood and appreciated their value and the value of diversity.

Seeing other dogs makes me realize the negative power of naming.
Like me, ALL dogs love to run and play more than anything else,
no matter what they're named.

I know I was only dreaming,
but I wish people could be a little more like dogs.

Naming can encourage, uplift, and honor;
but it can also put down, diminish, and make small.
Bob has decided to stay away from names
that keep him from loving who or what he sees.
He is sad to see how often he has made a big life small
by giving it a name that harbors negative judgment or mistrust.

Bob tells me that seeing the good in all things
large and small gives him kinder eyes and opens his heart.

THE FLAME

In the evening, it feels so good to sit with Bob
while he reads, writes, or watches TV.
But every once in a while as we're relaxing,
everything turns off and it gets dark.
Bob says, "Oh no, there goes the
electricity. . .again."

He seems upset, but I think it's nice.

Whenever that happens, Bob lights some
candles and sets them around the house.
They make me feel peaceful inside.

If I could, I would light a candle for you.
I want you to feel its warmth,
see its glow, and love its rhythm.
I want you to have it for those moments
when it's hard to see, when dreams fade,
and when the night seems like it will never end.
I want you to have it because everyone needs
the candle of kindness and compassion.

Everyone needs to know they are loved.

ABOUT ME, BOB LUCKIN

I was the second oldest of seven children born to a kindhearted American baptist mother of French ancestry. My father was the opposite: a severely abusive man who suffered from paranoid schizophrenia that hindered his ability to hold a steady job. He was placed in an orphanage after his Scottish immigrant parents died upon arrival in this country.

Our family lived in dirt-floored shacks, hotel rooms, small apartments, and neighborhoods where English was a second language and nearly everything was broken. Everyone I knew was poor. I wore Salvation Army clothes, ate government cheese, and drank powdered milk.

When it was safe I found solace in my imagination and old movies. I loved music and nature more than people. I began writing poetry at age seven, yet struggled in school, where I failed every subject taught in each of the ten or more schools I attended. I stuttered, was shy, and believed the teachers report that said I was lazy, slow, and best suited for a menial job. I quit school at sixteen, got a job in a factory, gave my paycheck to my mother, tried to save my $5 weekly allowance, then left home at seventeen knowing there had to be a better life.

It took me until the age of twenty-one to get my GED so I could go to college. I spent the first semester of college sitting in the parking lot watching students come and go to the class I had registered for but was unable to attend because of fear.

continued on page 96...

The second semester, I registered, again, attended, and failed. On my third try, the professor instructed me to write a two-thousand-word essay on the philosopher Nietzsche. After handing in my paper I watched with nearly a hundred other students as he pulled my paper from the pile and read it out loud. After finishing, he told the class my paper was the reason he taught college.

It was that moment that gave my life new meaning.

From then on, I passed all my college and university classes, got my degrees, and moved forward to achieve a positive and meaningful life as a husband, father, artist, college professor, writer, therapist, and ordained minister. I can't say it has been an easy life, but it has been a good one.